JULIET MUGOTI

SANGO reRIMUKA
Does Not Eat Its Own Children

A Stage Play In Two Acts

By

Alf E.F. Muronda

MASAKA PUBLISHING

ISBN   978-1-965398-33-3
© Elfigio F Muronda
Published by **MASAKA PUBLISHING MEDIA
HOUSE**
alf@cip7sisters.com

For Hilton Mambo, Mupamombe, Thank you for the inspiration.

TABLE OF CONTENTS

Sango reRimuka
Does Not Eat Its Own Children
A Stage Play In Two Acts

Thematic Overview

Set in Sadza District in rural Zimbabwe, the story unfolds in two days over a National Heroes Day weekend holiday. At its heart is *Sango reRimuka*, a sacred ancient forest which represents the cultural, spiritual, and ancestral heritage of the Mugoti family. Through various themes, the play confronts modern Africa's existential dilemmas. It weaves together themes of family, tradition, greed, and redemption focusing on Juliet, a woman whose actions jeopardize both her family's unity and the sanctity of *Sango reRimuka*.

CHARACTERS

Chigare Mugoti	Sekuru *(renowned herbalist)*
Phineas Mugoti MD	Sekuru's eldest son
Juliet Mugoti	Phineas' wife
Tichaona Mugoti	Sekuru's late middle son *(liberation war hero)*
Pondai Mugoti	Sekuru's youngest son
Kambezo Chibandi	Juliet's Business Partner
Zvanyadza	Pondai's wife
Elton	Phineas & Juliet's son 8 yrs son
Rudo & Chipo	Pondai & Zvanyadza's twin daughters 8 yrs old
Josphat	Mugoti family employee

INTRODUCTION

We are at Mugoti Village compound in Sadza District in rural Zimbabwe. It is Heroes Day a national holiday weekend celebrating the country's liberation forces. The holiday happens to have fallen on the weekend before the district's *"chisi"* (day of rest) which is the area's traditional equivalent to Christian people's Sunday - day of rest. The villagers around the Mugoti village are in the middle of celebrations preparing for a *bira* the night before *"chisi"* where they will come together to celebrate the country's heroes as well as their own community, family, good health, and the prosperity they enjoy from *Sango reRimuka*. **Chigare Mugoti,** the chief of the district, is the patriarch of the Mugoti family and a renowned *nganga* who is the principal healthcare provider for the villagers in the district.

Chigare Mugoti, known affectionately as Sekuru, is the steward/guardian of *Sango reRimuka*, an ancient forest reserve which encompasses most of the land around Mugoti Village and nineteen other villages that are dotted around its edges.

Sango reRimuka is more than land; it is legend. Its trees whisper the voices of ancestors, its soil guards riches seen and unseen. For generations, the firstborn son of the Mugoti family has inherited the title *Gamba reRimuka* —a sacred duty to safeguard the forest, ensuring its survival for the twenty villages that depend on its spirit and

7

sustenance. With that designation, all matters to do with the *Sango reRimuka* are left up to that person to protect the interests of *Sango reRimuka* for the good of all members of the community.

Sekuru Chigare Mugoti has three sons. **Phineas**, the eldest of three brothers, runs a medical practice in Harare and is confident that it provides well for his wife, **Juliet**, and their son, **Elton**. Phineas' family carries deep history. His middle brother, **Tichaona**, died fighting for the country's liberation, leaving behind a legacy of heroism. The youngest, **Pondai**, a bio-engineering graduate student, lives in the village close to their widowed father, Chigare Mugoti, raising twin daughters while pursuing his studies online.

For Mugoti family and the villagers, this weekend is a celebration of Tichaona, the fallen hero of the family and his comrades who liberated the country.

For Juliet Mugoti and her business partner, this weekend has the potential to make them a fortune that could turn their lives around, if only Sekuru Mugoti and his two sons will co-operate with their plan.

THE PLAY

Sango reRimuka
A place that exists somewhere in Our Motherland.

SANGO reRIMUKA
Does Not Eat Its Own Children

ACT One

Scene 1

Before the curtain opens, there is a sound of an automobile arriving. The sound of the automobile's engine is heard as it dominates the celebratory ululating and drumming and shouting going on behind the curtain.

"Welcome doctor!"

"Welcome Mupawose!"

The sound of the automobile's engine dies off as people continue to shout "Mauya!" Mauya!" "Mupawose!" "Chiremba na Elton!"

The curtain opens to reveal the interior of a house. We are in the living/dining room. The door opens and in comes Dr Phineas Mugoti, his wife Juliet and their 8-year-old son, Elton.

They have parcels and suitcases which they put down when they enter the room.

From outside the house, the audience will hear continuous sounds filtering into the house. These ambient sounds come from people talking, shouting, tuning their musical instruments, the drums, and the mbiras. References will be made to the people who are not seen by the audience but are sitting on the ground in the compound waiting to be seen by Sekuru Chigare Mugoti for their ailments.

Elton: Mummy you do not know where to go in this house. Let me show you, my room. I have a room here in Sekuru's house!"

Phineas: Yes, Elton lead the way, and show your mother where to put her bags!"

Juliet takes off her coat following behind her son and husband but stops to admire the living/dining room. She is looking around in awe.

Juliet: Oh, my, I cannot believe we are *kumusha* (rural village). Phineas, this house is simply beautiful. You wouldn't think you were in a rural village.

Phineas: Well, you can thank my younger brother Pondai and his wife for that. Pondai works with *baba* (father), and this is what they have done.

Juliet: I was last here 5 years ago when we came to bury your mother. Back then the house was just at the foundation level.

Elton *(interrupts):* Mum, mummy come and see my room, and the girls have their own room too, when they sleep here.

Juliet: Ok let me see. (*She disappears walking into the bedroom wing following the two.*)

The audience can hear Juliet as she continues to sing praises of the house.

Juliet: Really? Elton is this your room?

Elton: Yes, it's my room mum. Sekuru gave it to me!

Juliet: Sekuru must like you a lot!

Elton: Sekuru likes everybody, daddy and you have a room, Chipo and Rudo have their own room.

There is a sound of another automobile engine raving up and then dies. We hear a car door being closed.

There is a loud knock at the door.

Voice from outside: Knock, knock! *Mukoma* Phineas! Doctor! It's me, Kambezo!

Phineas comes to the door. And there stands Kambezo Chibandi, the late Tichaona's childhood best friend. Behind him in the village compound the noise and sounds of merriment continue.

Phineas: Kambezo where did you come from!

Kambezo: *(Acting overly friendly)* Hesi Mukoma *(giving Phineas a big hug).* *(In his left hand is a bag of groceries)* I was so happy to meet your wife two weeks ago, my *Mai guru* Juliet, at a business meeting in town! I am sure she told you. I also came by your house, you were at work but she told me you were coming *kumusha* this Heroes weekend and I said that would be perfect! And so here I am to see you my brother and the whole Mugoti family and to celebrate my best friend Comrade Tichaona who died to give us this freedom we enjoy in Zimbabwe!

Phineas: Come in, come in please take a seat.

Kambezo puts the bag of groceries on the table as he slides into one of the chairs around the dining table.

> Phineas: How long has it been? Why did you think of us all of sudden?
>
> Kambezo: Ha! don't say that brother, I think of you all the time. You are my family.

Juliet and Elton come into the dining/ living room.

> Juliet: I thought I heard your voice.

Kambezo leaps to his feet. Speaking as he gives her a big hug.

> Kambezo: *Mai guru!* I told you I was coming. This is my home.
>
> Phineas: Elton say hello to uncle Kambezo. He was your *baba mudiki* Tichaona's best friend!
>
> Kambezo: Come here you big boy. Come give your uncle Kambezo a big hug.
>
> Elton (*coming into Kambezo's embrace*): Did you know my uncle Tichaona? Was he a brave man?
>
> Kambezo: Tichaona was the bravest of all the boys, in these villages. Tichaona and I were not just friends, we were brothers. We were always together even when we were your age.
>
> Elton: Did you go to war with my uncle Tichaona?
>
> Kambezo (*snickers and shakes his head*): No. But I wish I had.
>
> Elton: What happened? Were you sick?

Kambezo: No. He just left. He didn't tell me; he didn't tell anybody. You know you remind me of him so much, let me sing you a song Tichaona and I used to sing playing in *Sango reRimuka*.

Kambezo stops for dramatic effect and plays a little drum roll on the table with his fingers.

Kambezo: You want to hear it?

Elton: Yes, I like to sing.

Kambezo: Great. When I sing the first part, you sing and repeat, "Jo!" "Jo" Got it?

Elton: Yes.

Kambezo: You start singing "Jo" "Jo" "Jo" and I will join you.

Elton (*singing*): Jo! Jo! Jo! Jo! Jo! Jo! Jo! Jo! Jo!

Kambezo: Jo Kinjo kiriki jo kinjo! Jo Kinjo kiriki jo kinjo! Jo Kinjo kiriki jo kinjo!

As Kambezo and Elton sing the song, Juliet and Phineas get sucked into the funny rhythm and join in singing repeating Jo Jo with Elton. Kambezo ad-libs words to the song on his part until everyone starts laughing from Kambezo's funny ad-libs.

Phineas: Kambezo, you have always been funny! But you always could sing too!

Elton: That's a fun song

Juliet: Yes, it is. You should learn to sing it so you can sing it with your friends as your uncle used to do.

Elton: When I grow up, I am going to be strong
and brave like my uncle Tichaona...

Phineas: We call him "the comrade".

Elton: Yes, I am going to be like Comrade
Tichaona, big and brave!

Juliet: Yes, you will my son!

Elton: And people will come to celebrate me on
Heroes Day, just as we have come here to
celebrate my uncle Tichaona.

They all clap their hands.

Kambezo: You look so much like your comrade
uncle. I am sure you are going to be big, and brave
like him. You know, the funny thing is, you also
look like your grandfather Sekuru. (*Kambezo shakes
his head laughing*).

Elton suddenly remembers and exclaims.

Elton: Ah! *Baba!* I must go see Sekuru. May I go?

Phineas: Yes you may..

Before Phineas could finish the sentence, Elton runs to the door.

Elton (*shouting as he bolts out of the door*): I am going
to let Sekuru know I am here.

Phineas: Run along.

Phineas turns to Juliet and Kambezo.

Phineas: Did you hear that boy? He said he is
going to tell Sekuru "he" is here. Not "we" are
here. (*He laughs*) When we come here, he simply

forgets that I came with him. It's all about Sekuru this, Sekuru that... (*He shakes his head proudly*).

Juliet: Where is Sekuru? Where is Elton going?

Phineas: You see all those people in the yard sitting in line? There are Sekuru's patients waiting for consultations.

Juliet: So, he is busy, Elton shouldn't be disturbing him.

Phineas: Uhm you have no idea. His grandfather will stop whatever he's doing to talk to his grandson and besides he likes it when Elton is around. He becomes his assistant.

Juliet: What? I hope you are not going to let Sekuru drag our son into being a *nganga*. (*She laughs*).

Phineas: That's up to the ancestors, my dear.

Juliet: You became a medical doctor not a *nganga*, why would you let our son become a *nganga*?

Phineas: I am not saying anything. Elton loves his grandfather, and his grandfather adores him, so I let them enjoy each other's company.

Kambezo: Your son is so lucky to have a grandfather and a father.

Juliet: But you said you come from a village around here, don't you have family there?

Phineas: Yes, Kambezo comes from here, but his people are scattered. There is hardly anyone in his village, is there? Maybe that's why we have not seen you in years.

Kambezo (*trying to change the subject*): Uhm I am thirsty, any bottled spring water in the house? I have some in my car outside. Let me go get it.

Phineas: No need for that we are well stocked in here we have water and other drinks in the cellar. That room in there.

Kambezo: No disrespect *mukoma*, I prefer my own spring water *hahahah*.

Kambezo leaves the room to go get his spring water.

Juliet: What was he talking about? Spring water is spring water, we have plenty of it in here. He is a real character, isn't he?

Phineas: Yes, he is. You started to tell me, how you met him and something about road improvements in Sadza District. I am afraid I was preoccupied with one of my patient's test-results so, I really didn't hear you.

Juliet: Ha! what's new? You never listen...

Phineas: Honey that's not fair. I do listen to you.

Juliet: Well at least you heard the important part about road improvements in Sadza District. This contract is going to pay me so much, it will put my public relations firm on the map in Harare. With that money I can hire personal assistants and have my own office in town near my clients' offices. Can you imagine, $25,000 per kilo meter of any new roads constructed in Sadza District on top of the $15,000 engagement fee I received for my expenses when I signed the contract? This time I have hit the big one. Seeing as I am married to the Mugoti family, the work I have to do to earn my fees should not be that hard. So, I am here to work.

Phineas: I don't know what that's about but what's this I hear you say, "I am here to work"? I thought you said you wanted to come with me and Elton to the "rural village" this time because it's Heroes Holiday to celebrate my brother?

Juliet: Of course, of course, we are here for Comrade Tichaona.

Phineas: That's right, so what work are you talking about? *(Phineas asks the question getting up.)* The word "work" made me tired from all that driving, let me get us some snacks while we wait for my brother Pondai and his brood to come fix you something to eat.

Juliet: I can fix it myself but while you are at, it please bring me something too.

Phineas leaves the room to go get the snacks and Kambezo returns with his bottle of water and sits down.

Juliet: You started to tell me you are from here, where exactly are you from?

Kambezo (*shifting in his seat*): The truth is I grew up in this compound in this village. People use to think I was a Mugoti child. We were so poor, there was hardly ever any food at home, so I just played with Tichaona. I ate and slept here with the boys. I became one of Sekuru's sons. What happened is that when I was very young, younger than your son, my father was kicked by a donkey he was trying to put a yoke on. The donkey kicked him while he was turned around, so he didn't see it coming. He went up from the force of the kick and broke his leg. He never recovered from that. He became sick and lived in constant pain.

Juliet: And your mother?

Kambezo: I do not know. I think she went back to her home.

Juliet: And you?

Kambezo: At that time, I didn't know anything, but I adopted this family. Sekuru treated me like his own son Tichaona. And Ambuya, Tichaona's mother, was the kindest woman I have ever known.

Juliet: I have been married to Phineas for ten years, how come I never saw you before?

Kambezo: Well, it's a long story but the thing is, when Tichaona left to go to war. I was lost.

Juliet: Why didn't you follow him?

Kambezo: I do not know. I just left this village too and went to Harare and joined a *sungura* band. I got lost there.

Phineas returns with snacks and gives Juliet a bottle of spring water.

Phineas: So, Kambezo. It's been years. How did you two meet?

Kambezo: It's the ancestors *mukoma*. I didn't even know you were married. I was at a meeting two weeks ago trying to do a deal for road construction here in Sadza District when we met.

Juliet: Mupawose, *(Phineas' totem)* you know my ex-classmate from law school, Melania. Well, her law firm gave me the p.r. contract. I told you about it when I got the contract, but you were not listening. They have asked me to do some p.r. work on behalf of their client, a construction company that is working on a contract to build new roads in Sadza District.

Kambezo: I am with that company, McDougal & Son.

Phineas: I thought you were a musician. When did you go into the road construction business?

Kambezo: This music business is so-so, and my voice isn't that good anymore. I am doing different things now. I get tenders and joint venture with different companies and people in mining, road construction, any kind of tender I can get. I just do deals *mukoma*.

Phineas: Oh, I see.

Juliet: So, this company has a contract to upgrade the roads in Sadza District because of the damage from mining trucks and all that heavy equipment. You saw how bad the road was driving here.

Phineas: Yes, the roads could use some upgrade. So, what's the problem if the district and this company have an agreement.

Kambezo: There is no problem. It's just that as part of the agreement there is also a proposal to build new roads.

Juliet: They want to build new roads to help the villages around here.

Phineas: Well, they should go ahead and do that.

Kambezo: Well, the big road they propose to build is here but there is a problem with Sekuru.

They want to build a major road through *Sango reRimuka*.

Phineas: What? Why?

Juliet: To improve traffic.

Phineas: To improve what traffic, dear? Traffic going where? There is no traffic here.

Juliet: I do not know where exactly, but it is needed.

Phineas: Needed by whom?

Kambezo: *Mukoma* a new road will help this village.

Phineas: Am I missing something here? How will a road through *Sango reRimuka* help this village? Besides having to build a bridge across Rimuka River there's that great, big solid granite stone Mupawose Mountain and there is nothing for miles behind that mountain. Suppose you get over that mountain, what are you building a road for? Going where? You grew up here Kambezo, you know that forest is enchanted. It is the life blood of all our villages. It should not be disturbed.

Kambezo: I know but there is a lot of money to be made.

Phineas: Money to be made by who?

Before Kambezo can answer the door opens ushering in the drum music and external sounds. Pondai, Phineas' younger brother, his

24

wife Zvanyadza and their 8-year-old twins Chipo and Rudo burst through the door. The twins wrap themselves around their uncle Phineas while their mother embraces Juliet, her sister-in-law. Pondai greets Kambezo.

Pondai: We heard the car and rushed over but *mukoma* there are so many people out there in our compound. We had to stop and greet them all otherwise it would be disrespectful.

Juliet *(jokingly):* So, you girls love your uncle more than *meee*?

Phineas: Honey, forgive them. These girls last saw you 5 years ago when they were 3 years old. They see me and Elton often enough, they know us.

Juliet: Never mind, you two girls are so pretty. Beautiful girls.

Phineas: Girls say hello to your *mai guru* aunty Juliet.

Pondai: Ah look who is here? *Mukoma* Kambezo what a surprise! You are the last person I expected to see here today! But it's good to see you, big brother.

Kambezo: Hahaha I am glad to be here with you all young brother!

Pondai *(introducing his wife to Kambezo)*: *Mukoma* this is my wife, *Amai va* Chipo.

Zvanyadza: Glad to meet you *baba mukuru*.

Zvanyadza claps her hands in greeting and turns her attention back to Juliet.

The twins embrace their aunt Juliet. The twins both speak at once together.

>Twins: Where is Elton? Where is Elton?

>Phineas: You know where is. He is with your grandfather.

The twins bolt out of the house to go find their cousin Elton.

Pondai greets Juliet warmly and sits down:

>Kambezo: Pondai how have you been, young brother? Do you still live here?

>Pondai: I am ok *mukoma*. Yes, I live here, it is slow but healthy.

>Kambezo (*laughing*): Slow is good.

>Zvanyadza: You must be hungry after that long drive from Harare, let me go start preparing the food. Sekuru did not eat lunch, so I know, he will be hungry when he does finish with his patients.

(*Lights out*)

(*Lights on*)

Scene 2

Zvanyadza goes to the kitchen followed by Juliet.

>Juliet: Let me help you *amai nini*.

26

Zvanyadza: There isn't much to do. The twins already helped me with the preparations, so just relax.

Juliet looks around the kitchen.

Juliet: Woaw! You have a big refrigerator and a four-plate stove in this house, in this rural village! It's like you live in town or you live even better than people in the townships where I grew up.

Zvanyadza smiles proudly.

Zvanyadza: The refrigerator runs on solar power and the stove is gas. But sometimes we cook outside to save on gas or when it's too hot in here.

Juliet: I would not have believed it if I had not seen it for myself. So, with all these conveniences it means you have a lot of free time on your hands. How do you spend it? Where do you go?

Zvanyadza: The twins keep us busy. Sekuru needs help with the house and Pondai helps him with his patients when they pay. Some pay in cash, but you know, a lot of his people pay him with chickens, or goats or promises to pay later *(she laughs)*. Someone has to take care of that.

Juliet *(joins in the laughter):* Chickens and goats...

Zvanyadza: It's a lot of chickens too and sometimes a calf...when people are grateful to Sekuru; they can be very, very generous. *(She turns to admire Juliet's dress)* I like your dress. Can I feel the material?

Juliet: Sure. Phineas bought it for me when we were in Dubai last week.

Zvanyadza: Dubai? Like Dubai, Dubai? You went to Dubai?

Juliet: Yes. Being married to a doctor has its benefits, you know.

Zvanyadza: Uhm I cannot see myself in a place like Dubai.

Juliet: Why not? You know my husband told me his brother; your husband Pondai got 15 points at A level. He has Biology, Physics and Chemistry. He is still young he can go to medical school too. What school would not accept someone with such high marks?

Zvanyadza: Pondai is busy with his father and the twins. Besides he is studying bioengineering by correspondence, online.

Juliet: I do not know how much he can make with that but being a medical doctor is a ticket to Dubai.

Zvanyadza bursts out laughing.

Zvanyadza: Uhm I don't think Pondai cares about Dubai.

Juliet: But you should. You are both still young. He can do it. And you are lucky you are already married to a husband who is so smart he could be a medical doctor. So, you could become a doctor's wife. You know growing up I did a lot of fashion shows and beauty pageants hoping to meet a "Mr. Right" with money to take care of me. I did that until I wised up and studied hard and got admitted to the law school at the university. At university I met the right guy, a doctor. Doctors are the best husbands.

Zvanyadza bursts out laughing again.

Zvanyadza: Amai guru you went to university just to meet a doctor to marry you?

Juliet laughs too as she responds.

Juliet: You want me to lie? Yes of course. I was not going to remain poor living in a 2-bedroom tiny house in Highfields with my mother and brother and be enrolled in law school. I got pregnant and dropped out of law school and got married. People put themselves in the right place to get what they want. Men, women we all do that. Sadly, I miscarried that pregnancy and two after that. *(She pauses.)* But, hey, this is not about me. It's about you and Pondai. You must get out of this rural village. There is nothing for you here. He

29

is so smart. You two can do much better than this, living out here in a rural village is for losers.

Zvanyadza: Pondai has some business ideas of his own. Besides, he loves it here. Maybe the twins may want to do medicine but not Pondai. You know he has taught the twins coding. There is very little that Rudo does not know about computing and coding. She loves I.T., and Pondai is very proud of that. But Chipo likes people and animals so maybe she can become a doctor or veterinarian.

Juliet: Well, I will just have to talk to Pondai myself about this. He has too much brains to waste them living out here in the sticks.

Zvanyadza: You can try but I can tell you, he is happy here.

Phineas calls from the dining room.

Phineas: *Amai nini,* are there any more chips or peanuts in the house?

Zvanyadza: Yes, I will get you some?

Juliet: Let me take care of that, we brought some too. There are munchies in one of the paper bags on the table, he just did not look.

Zvanyadza: Ok but you didn't have to bring any more food with you. *Baba mukuru* Phineas built himself a small cold room in the other room, you can find anything you need in there.

Juliet: Uhm we even have cold rooms in the village. No wonder he likes coming here.

Scene 3

Back in the dining room where Phineas, Pondai and Kambezo are sitting, Juliet places a bowl of potato chips and peanuts on the table.

Juliet: *Baba mudiki,* can I get you something, coke or orange juice?

Pondai: No thank you. I will just help myself to one of these bottles of water. (*Pondai speaks as he reaches for a bottle of water from the table,*)

Someone shouts through the window.

Voice: Is there anyone in the house?

Pondai: Yes, we are here.

Voice: Sekuru said to leave this goat with you.

Pondai: Josphat is not out there?

Voice: No, there is no one out here.

Pondai: Okay I will come and get it.

Pondai leaves the room.

Juliet: Honey this place is so busy?

Phineas: It is Heroes Holiday weekend. Sekuru always invites people from all over the district to celebrate the comrades. Tichaona was his favourite.

Kambezo: That is so true. He loved Tichaona so much. When Sekuru found out that Tichaona had left to join the guerrillas, he was not the same for some time. He used to call me to sit with him but both of us were lost in our own thoughts missing Tichaona. And this place was no longer the same without Tichaona.

Phineas *(cheerfully)*: But now you should hear Sekuru describe Tichaona's heroism in battle. You'd think he was there with him.

Kambezo: Maybe he was there with him. You know Sekuru has powers. He is clairvoyant too.

Phineas: Boy don't I know it? Growing up around my father was hard, he could always tell if any of us had been up to no good.

Juliet*(laughing)*: You, being up to no good? *Baba va* Elton uhm *eh ehe*.

Kambezo: I probably shouldn't say this in front of you *Mai guru* Juliet but Mukoma Phineas was…

Phineas *(jokingly threatens)*: KAMBEZO!

Juliet *(still laughing)*: Let him tell me.

At that moment Elton and the twins suddenly come back in. Elton is excited.

Elton: Mummy, this is the best part about *kumusha*. Rudo, Chipo and I are going to pick wild berries like *maroro* and *tsambatsi*.

Juliet: Where?

Elton: *Sango reRimuka* of course…

Zvanyadza shouts from the kitchen.

Zvanyadza: No one is going anywhere until you three come in here and finish peeling these potatoes.

Chipo: That's nothing. Elton come on, let's do it.

The three children troop into the kitchen to peel the potatoes.

Juliet: I have not seen Elton this excited at home. He is even helping in the kitchen.

Phineas: He loves his grandfather and his cousins.

Juliet: I am sorry I could only give you this one child.

Phineas: It's not your fault, besides we are happy as a family as we are, so leave it alone.

Juliet: Ok but if Elton is going to play outside, he must put his hat on.

The three children troop back into the dining room.

Juliet: You finished peeling the potatoes already?

Elton: There were only 4 potatoes left.

Juliet: Go get your hat. I do not want you going outside without it.

Elton: Why mummy?

Kambezo: Because your mother said so.

Juliet: Yes, that's right, it's because I said so, that's why.

Elton: Ok.

When the three children are leaving the house, we hear Elton tell the girls that he is not wearing a hat if they are not wearing hats. The twins tell him to just pretend to wear it and leave it on a tree outside the yard and put it back on when they return.

When Pondai opens the door to come back into the house, a heavy dose of drumming explodes into the house from the yard outside.

Juliet: That drumming is amazing. Who is that playing those drums.

Phineas: Wait till tomorrow. This is just a warmup. These local boys can beat that drum until it cries, *mother!* You know Juliet my dear, in your own way, you are just as excited to be here as Eton is. *(He laughs)*

Juliet: But I am afraid of spiders, bugs and wild animals, you know that is why I do not come here *kumusha* with you when you come with Elton.

Phineas: I know but have you seen any spiders in here?

Juliet: No that's why I keep saying it's like I am not even in a rural village.

Kambezo: There is nothing wrong with a rural village, is there?

Juliet: Well, yes, nothing happens in a rural village except bugs and snakes…

Phineas: She is exaggerating.

They all laugh.

Juliet pauses as the drums continue to thunder from outside.

Juliet: Growing up in Highfields in the townships of Harare, we never really had pure authentic African drums like that.

Pondai: There is something about the African drum and the mbira that comes through to your heart when you play them in their native environment away from the glare of the lights and the noise of motor cars you hear in towns.

Juliet: Yes. I can feel it.

Kambezo: Tichaona and I grew up in the middle of that. He knew how to beat that drum and I would sing, making up our songs. Oh, how I miss him.

They are all quiet momentarily listening to the rhythm of the drum.

Juliet: So, *baba mudiki* Pondai, what happened to the goat you were called out for. You were not gone that long?

Pondai: Josphat takes care of the goats. He was outside where he was supposed to be. He just had not seen the man with the goat.

Kambezo is quiet, listening to the beat of the drummers, nodding off in his own world.

Juliet: So, what happens to the goats and the chickens that my sister-in-law was telling me you collect from all Sekuru's patients who cannot pay in cash?

Pondai: Actually, a lot of people *baba* sees do not have any cash nor any livestock to pay but *baba* does not mind.

Juliet: He gives them his medicines for free?

Pondai: *Baba* does not think of himself as the one who actually does the healing. He says most people can heal themselves through the mind with the aid of herbs that come from *Sango reRimuka*.

Juliet: So how do you make a living or even become wealthy if you give away your services for free? I cannot see Phineas doing that at his surgery in Harare. We would go broke, and we would starve to death.

Phineas: I think *baba* has always done okay financially. He took care of the education costs for both of us. Pondai and I, we both went to boarding schools from Form One to Form Six with *baba* paying our fees.

Juliet: But still, I think he would do better financially if he did not give away his services for free as you are saying.

Pondai: *Baba* does not pay for medicinal supplies. Everything he uses to help the people he helps comes from *Sango reRimuka*. The plants, trees, and herbs he uses are all free.

Juliet: Then I assume, you have accumulated lots of goats and chickens and cattle in the pens?

Pondai: No, we have some but every other week I take some livestock to Sadza Township on Fridays and sell them to the butcheries or to people coming from town on the buses.

Zvanyadza sticks her head out from the kitchen and speaks.

Zvanyadza: The food is ready; I should have made the children set the table.

Juliet: Not to worry. *Baba mudiki* Pondai, show me where she keeps the plates, and I will take care of it.

Pondai: Right behind you, in the closed cupboard on the wall. I will help you.

Juliet (*exclaims*): Oh my! Zvanyadza! *Amai nini*, you have full sets of china!

Zvanyadza (*from the kitchen):* It's just for special guests. Sekuru insists that when *Mukoma* Phineas comes home, he is the head of our family. *Gamba reRimuka* must be served like a king.

Juliet: He is a king at our house too, but we do not serve him every meal on special china.

Phineas: No, she does not.

They all laugh as Juliet sets the table. Zvanyadza comes out of the kitchen with the food and sets it on the table. They wash and clap their hands thankfully and start eating. As they eat Juliet asks.

Juliet: Shouldn't we call the children in to eat?

Phineas: Elton and the girls eat whenever they come back. In fact, I imagine they are not hungry right now. They are feasting on the fruits from *Sango reRimuka*, they prefer that to home cooked food.

Kambezo: Just like we used to when we were their age.

Pondai: Even I too used to do that too, just eat *Rimuka* forest berries and forget about coming home to eat.

Juliet: And Sekuru? When does he come in to eat?

Pondai: We leave his food in the oven. He will not eat dinner until he has seen his last patient, which is any time after the sun starts going down. We will take his food to him. When he works long like today, he sleeps out there in his rondevale. He says he does not want to bring the spiritual burdens he carries from the day's patients into the house. He will come back into the house tomorrow.

Juliet: But today is Sunday. Why is he at work? Besides it being the National Heroes holiday weekend, Sunday is a day of rest.

Pondai: Not here in our villages and the surrounding district. Our day of rest, which is called *"chisi"* is Tuesday. That is when we rest. No one goes to work; we just rest like it's your Sunday.

Juliet: I have never heard of that. Why do you people around these parts do that?

Phineas: I grew up with it. Sunday as a day of rest was imposed on us by the Christian missionaries and their compatriots the European colonizers. Our people here try to honour their ancestral traditions.

Juliet: But why not just rest on Sunday like everyone else?

Pondai: The Jews are not resting on Sunday. Neither are the Muslims, the Chinese, and many other cultures.

Juliet: Still, you are not Jews or Muslims...

Phineas: *Amai va* Elton that would assume that everyone here is a Christian, which is not true. Besides, it just so happens that us, Africans, in this part of the world follow what we follow simply because we are victims of what you could say are the 3 Cs. Colonialization, Capitalism and Christianity. Those three Cs go together and they explain our recent history. Personally, I do not know how holy Sunday is, but I do know that it is convenient for churches and businesses for it to be the way it is.

Juliet (*sheepishly with a smile*): I never thought of Sunday as being anything other than just being Sunday.

Pondai: *Amai guru* you are not the only one. Most of us Africans seem to have no idea we had a culture before what *mukoma* Phineas calls the 3 Cs.

Zvanyadza: But people know that Sekuru does not see patients on Tuesday, the day of *chisi* so it is usually very busy here during the weekend. Besides tomorrow night is *bira* so Sekuru will spend the whole day just resting so he can be up all night.

As they eat, they continue to talk.

Juliet: So *amai nini* Zvanyadza tell me, why do all these people come here to Sekuru? Is it because his services are free?

Zvanyadza: Uhm I do not think so. People with broken bones and some other ailments do not come here.

Juliet: Where do they go?

Zvanyadza: To the clinic at Sadza Township.

Juliet: So, who comes here to Sekuru?

Phineas: All kinds of people from all over the country, not just the local villagers; people travel from as far away as Uzumba to come to be seen by Sekuru Chigare Mugoti.

Phineas shakes his head and pauses.

Phineas: You know, throughout most of my years in boarding school. I was ashamed to tell people that I was a son of a *nganga*. The mission school priests and nuns all of them had something horrible to say about *ngangas and svikiros*. Anything to do with our native Zimbabwe culture including our names was of the devil. All of it was labelled as bad, bad, bad barbaric. I was so intimidated.

Pondai: I am glad I did not go to a missionary boarding school, so I did not have to have a European name.

Juliet: What about European names?

Phineas: My father had to give me a European person's name in order for me to be accepted for enrolment in that missionary school.

Pondai: I once asked *amai* why they gave you the name Phineas because there is no one in our family history with that name.

Phineas: No there is no one called Phineas in our family history, and I hope I am the first and last.

Zvanyadza (*pleading*): Uhm do not say that *baba mukuru*, the twins admire you. They may want to name their child "Phineas" in honour and memory of you.

Phineas: You see that's the problem with the 3 Cs. We are stuck with their legacy. Our son Elton is named in honour of his maternal and paternal grandfathers. Elton's full name is Elton Chigare Mugoti. People may not want to give their children European names but if you love someone in your family and you want to preserve their memory you will have no choice but name them the Jack, James or Phineas or whatever because of it. Unlike the Indians and other Asians who refused to give up their culture and names when they were subjugated by the Europeans, our people submitted. It's something to think about on this holiday when we are celebrating the heroes who liberated us from colonization.

Phineas takes a sip from a glass of water as he eats and continues.

Phineas: As educated as I am, I cannot believe it took me this long to appreciate what people like my father, the village healers, the *ngangas*, mean to the healthcare of our people here and in Africa in

42

general. And for me it all started with that missionary school indoctrination ingrained in me against our culture. There was so much negativity cast upon it, you could not see anything good about our culture even if it's in your face. One of the reasons why I bring Elton here to spend time with his grandfather as often as I do is because in a way, I want to make up for the years I was not proud of the work that my father does.

Juliet: What do you mean? When I met you, you did not seem to be ashamed of your father.

Phineas: I just never showed it, but it's been a gradual process. When I became a doctor and started seeing patients on my own, I also began to see that medicine is more than just pills and prescriptions, something they did not dwell too much on in medical school during my time there.

Sounds from the drumming and people shouting filter into the room causing Phineas to pause.

Phineas *(continues)*: Many things have happened that have made me look at my father and those who practice indigenous traditional medicines differently. For example, one day I heard *baba* talking to a young patient, a boy who was about 12 years old, who was suffering from migraine headaches. He had come here with his father.

Pondai: *Baba* has an effective herbal cure for migraine headaches.

Phineas: Yes, I have since found that out and we shall talk about that. Anyway, *baba* gave the boy the herbal powder which the boy was to drink as a tea for a week. But what I found to be strange was when he asked the boy if he was right-handed or left-handed. The boy said he was right-handed and *baba* told him to wash his face with his left hand for that week.

Everyone laughs.

Phineas *(laughing too):* Wait, wait you think it's funny but listen to this. After the boy and his father were gone, I asked *baba* why he had told the boy to wash his face with his left hand. In response to my question *baba* explained that he was trying to disrupt whatever was in his young mind that was bringing on the migraines. Because the boy was not used to using his left hand, *baba* said, doing so would require him to focus on that and also reinforce the sense that the herbal tea works that way. I know that *baba's* herbal powder works on headaches regardless, but I was struck by the psychological component of his diagnosis and prescription. It sounds simplistic but hey, whatever works.

Everyone is quiet contemplating on what Phineas has just said.

Phineas: So over time that exchange with *baba* and other things, I have experienced personally as a practicing doctor, have made me realize that a *nganga* is not some mindless *"ugabuga"* as the missionaries tried to drill into my head. A good and true *nganga* like *baba* is "a practitioner of indigenous African medicines and psychiatry"

Pondai: I like that. Our father Chigare Mugoti is a Practitioner of African Medicines & Psychiatry. I am going to get him cards printed with his professional title written just the way you said it.

Phineas*(laughing):* And who is he going to give those cards to?

Juliet: His patients, of course *(laughing too).*

The laughter explodes.

Juliet: Speaking of business cards, *baba mudiki* Pondai, wouldn't you like to see the initials MD after your own name, like your brother Phineas?

Pondai: You mean like medical doctor?

Juliet: Yes, you are so smart. You got 15 points in Physics, Chemistry and Biology. You are a natural to go to medical school.

Phineas: *Amai va* Elton you are 7 years too late honey. I tried to encourage him to go that route, but he said no.

Juliet: Why not? It's not too late. All he has to do is commit a few years of his young life to medical school and he will be like you, an MD.

Pondai: *Amai guru* you see that tv monitor behind you? It's not just a tv, it's a classroom for me as well as the twins. I hook up my laptop to that monitor and off I go into cyber space. I am studying bioengineering online. And I find that I am pretty good at it.

Juliet: So, what are you going to do with a bioengineering degree out here in this rural village? As a doctor you can practice anywhere you chose.

Pondai: There is a lot I intend to do with my bioengineering degree here in this rural community. Today's technology makes it easy and possible to study whatever you want, wherever you want. My place is here with *baba* and *Sango reRimuka*. There is much to be done here.

Juliet: From what I hear *Sango reRimuka* is a piece of underdeveloped land that you and this rural community need developed, something which you cannot possibly do by yourselves.

Pondai: Who said anything about *Sango reRimuka* needing development? *Sango reRimuka* is about as close to paradise as you can get *amai guru*. It is perfect. It needs no development.

Juliet: I hear there is a need for roads and bridges to go through that forest.

Kambezo: Yes good, good, tarred roads.

Pondai: I do not know who you heard from, but the district council people tried to con us into believing that a new road through our forest is something we needed.

Phineas: Pondai, hold up a minute. This is something I was not aware of. Earlier this afternoon when we arrived, your *Amai guru* Juliet and Kambezo surprised me with the news that they both are working for a company that is contracted to improve roads in Sadza District with a particular purpose to build a major road to run through *Sango reRimuka*.

Pondai: Did I hear you right? *Mukoma*, you are saying that *mukoma* Kambezo is part of the plan that is supposed to build a road in *Sango reRimuka?*

Kambezo: Yes. I am working with McDougal & Son to upgrade roads in Sadza District and build new roads through *Sango reRimuka*.

Pondai: I am surprised that it is you. Are you serious?

Juliet: Of course, he is serious, why not?

Pondai: This is sad, is all I can say. And you *Amai guru* you also work for the same compony?

Juliet: Uhm not directly but I am doing the p.r. work.

Pondai: So, you both came here today of all days, after all these years, on Tichaona's Heroes celebration day, to tell us you are part of the project to desecrate what is sacred and untouchable?

Pondai shakes his head.

Juliet *(defensively):* What do mean desecrate? We are just businesspeople.

Kambezo *(sheepishly):* Yes, it is just business.

Juliet *(lamely):* We are just trying to make some money?

Phineas *(incredulously):* By turning this community upside down?

Kambezo *(in a weak voice barely above a whisper):* *Mukoma* this is progress.

Pondai: Obviously you do not get it. Let me ask you this, *Mukoma* Kambezo you say you are with McDougal & Son company, how are you with this company?

Kambezo: What do you mean?

Pondai: Are you a shareholder, a partner, an employee or what?

Kambezo: I am a partner in this deal.

Pondai: Ok as a partner have you seen and read the contract between McDougal & Son company and Sadza District.

Kambezo: The deal is to build roads.

Phineas: He asked you, as a partner have you seen and read the agreement document?

Kambezo: Well actually no. I just know what the deal is.

Pondai: So, you think you know what the deal is?

Unsure of himself, Kambezo nods his head.

Phineas: Juliet, what is your contract for? What did you sign to do?

Juliet: To get the villagers and Sekuru to understand progress. Upgrade the roads and build a new major road though *Sango reRimuka*.

Pondai (*incredulous*): Uhm so this is why you are visiting us today? (*He laughs*) I was about to get very, very angry and disrespectful but my spirit tells me that this is not worth my anger, and it is not my fight. I am sorry I must laugh because you are both out of your minds to say the least.

Juliet: Why? What is so funny?

Pondai: It is obvious to me that both of you are in over your heads. I am sure you do not even know what the wording of the contract between

McDougal and Sadza District is and what it gives McDougal the right to do.

Phineas: Kambezo, after all those years you lived here with us as a son of this house, did you learn anything about our way of life and what is sacred?

Kambezo: Yes, I did *mukoma* and I am grateful.

Pondai: *Mukoma* Kambezo I am younger than you so I might not understand. But is it that now that you live in the big city you do not respect our ways, our traditions, and customs?

Juliet: What customs and traditions? I am a Christian. Business is business.

Pondai: Understand this *Mai guru* Juliet. *Sango reRimuka* is as alive as you and I are. For your information *Sango reRimuka* does not care about your religion. In fact, it knows not what a Christian or a Muslim is and neither do I. The only thing *Sango reRimuka* knows is the difference between friend and foe. That forest has survived and has been here since before our time, I dare say McDougal, you, *mai guru* Juliet, *mukoma* Kambezo and the corrupt Sadza District officers are light weights. *Sango reRimuka* will defend itself, so tread carefully. You are stirring a hornet's nest. From what I can tell, the contracts you signed are not worth the paper they are written on.

50

Juliet: But what is wrong with doing business.

Pondai: You do not get it, do you, *mai guru*? There is no business for you and McDougal & Son here in *Sango reRimuka*. None. Actually I am finding it hard to accept that two people who are affiliated with this Mugoti family, people who do not even live here, have a financial interest in ripping our *Sango reRimuka* apart.

Juliet: No *baba mudiki* Pondai, no one is here to rip anything apart. There is nothing strange in that we have financial interests, that's how business is done. Business is based on relationships.

Pondai: I see the "relationships". It is obvious that because of "relationships" as you say, someone inside Sadza District council administration recruited you both on the basis of your relationship to the Mugoti family to get to Sekuru because everything else they have tried has not worked.

Kambezo: I get tenders from district councils all the time, this is no different.

Pondai: You are my elder brother Kambezo and *mai guru* Juliet so I will tell you the facts as plain as I can make them. But I must say, I did not expect this from within the family.

Phineas: Personally, I am quite baffled. I never thought something as outrageous as this would come from you, Kambezo. It may be understandable coming from Juliet because she does not know anything about the deadly flesh wound you are trying to inflict on the soil of our ancestors but not you Kambezo. You have no excuse for this outrageous proposition that has brought you back here to our home after all these years.

Juliet: *Baba va* Eliot, what is so outrageous about the plan of trying to build a road in this god forsaken rural place?

Pondai: Out of respect for you as my *mai guru,* and as my brother, your husband said, you may be forgiven because you do know not anything about us and our land.

Phineas: I am thinking this did not just pop out of nowhere.

Pondai: No, it did not.

Phineas: So, you are not as surprised as I am.

Pondai: No. I am not *mukoma.* Some time ago the officers from Sadza District came to see Sekuru with someone who was introduced as a road construction contractor. The officers from the Sadza District offices were excited this contractor

52

was going to upgrade the roads in Sadza District for almost next to nothing. It was next to nothing because all the other contractor/bidders for the contract to upgrade Sadza District roads had quoted actual cost prices for such a job.

Phineas: Uhm I see, go on.

Pondai: They told *baba* they had awarded the contract to this company because that company was going to build new roads in the district also at rock bottom prices.

Phineas: New roads from where to where and for what purpose?

Pondai: They did not say except that for the contractor to make any profit from all this generous work he was going to do for the district, he had to build a new road into *Sango reRimuka*.

Phineas: You say, he "had" to build a new road in *Sango reRimuka* particularly? Why *Sango reRimuka*? Going where?

Pondai: They did not give us much information except to say that it was needed and our village was going to make a lot of money

Kambezo: I told you *mukoma* Phineas, there is a lot of money to made.

Phineas: By who?

Kambezo: Everybody.

Pondai: Sekuru allowed them to make their presentation. He did not say yes or no. He told them they would be a meeting of all the villages on the matter.

Phineas: A meeting to decide what? He should have just told them to go and not come back.

Pondai: It was quite upsetting but Sekuru does not do things on his own. As the chief and steward/guardian of *Sango reRimuka*, he called all the heads and families of the twenty villages together to talk about it and we all decided against it. There are enough big roads all around us, we do not need another one in here. In fact, we do not think that it is about building us a road or bridge, which we did not ask for. They think we are simple minded villagers who are not aware that the belt of gold that starts from Murowa Mountain runs through *Sango reRimuka*. That is what that is about. It's not about building roads. It is about mining gold.

Juliet: So, what is wrong with gold mining? You all can get very wealthy if you partner with gold mining companies to mine that gold in *Sango reRimuka*.

Phineas: Juliet everything cannot be just about money.

Pondai: *Amai guru* before we talk any further about your mission here and how it will affect us, the people who live in these villages, let me tell you something about the world outside of *Sango reRimuka*. *(Pondai drinks some water and clears his throat.)* I am sure you have heard about the global warming issue and climate change. You know how it started?

Juliet: No.

Pondai: It started with the industrial revolution in Europe, in the UK to be precise. And just so you are aware, Africa was not a beneficiary of the Industrial Revolution. Africa was and still is a victim of the industrial revolution. European nations plundered their own forests and their natural resources. But that was not enough, there is never enough for the captains of industry. They set their sights on us and our resources. They forcibly came to Africa with guns, captured and made us their slaves and divvied up Africa into countries for the natural resources to build up their own countries. In the process of industrialization, they polluted their own bodies of water and air. A few centuries later, the chickens have come home to roast - European, American and Chinese air is polluted hence climate change. That same polluted air has drifted all over the world including our own African skies. Now that polluted air filled with carbon dioxide is causing climate changes in Africa causing environmental devastations on poor African communities which had nothing to do with the industrial revolution in first place. This mining and wanton industrialization are part of the bedrock of modern economies which run this world. I am not naïve to think that we, here at *Sango reRimuka* villages, can stop climate change or any of that. However, we do know that a mining company coming to *Sango reRimuka* will tear up the land to extract what they want from the ground and disrupt the ecology. The plants and herbs that *baba* uses for medicinal herbs will be trampled under by graders and bull dozers. Our hunting grounds will vanish overnight. Rimuka River which feeds us with fish, provides us with drinking water as well as where we wash our clothes, and our bodies will become a murky pool. Then worst of all, *makorokoza* who follow the big mining companies will come into our community to pan for gold from the river and next thing you know, it's no longer safe to walk day or night around here. No *amai guru*, we are already mining something much bigger than gold here; we have everything we need without disrupting the paradise our ancestors bequeathed us. I know that as long as Sekuru is alive he will not allow it and I hope that we, his children, and our children and their children will also maintain and protect *Sango reRimuka* for the good of all.

Juliet (*with a big sigh*): Oh, I see.

Phineas' phone rings. He retrieves it from his pocket and stands up.

Phineas: Excuse me, let me take this call.

Pondai continues the conversation with Juliet, Kambezo and Zvanyadza.

Pondai: I do not see how our community can benefit from any deal with your mining company that is hiding behind the title "road construction contractor" offering to build a road into *Sango reRimuka* for free. Mining companies are not charitable organizations. If they build any roads, it is because they need the roads for themselves to conduct their business. It follows therefore that your McDougal & Son will build a road for a purpose. What purpose? You tell me *mukoma* Kambezo. Why do they want to build a road we do not need?

Kambezo looks down. He has no answer.

There is a knock at the open window.

Voice: It's Josphat *baba*. Sekuru is seeing his last patent. Can I go?

Pondai: Okay. You can go and close the pens.

Voice: Okay, will do.

Phineas returns to the table.

Juliet *(jokingly)*: Doctor who is calling you on Sunday when the office is closed?

Phineas: That was my old friend Dr Mukiwa Kwesi.

Juliet: Isn't he in New York?

Phineas: Yes, he is a VP at MCK Pharma.

Juliet *(laughing)*: Are we flying to New York to visit your old college roommate?

Phineas: Uhm maybe *(joining Juliet in laughter)*.

Zvanyadza stands to clear the table.

Phineas: I do not know what is going to happen to your doing business in *Sango reRimuka*, Sekuru will be here in the house tomorrow Kambezo. You can take up the matter with him.

Pondai: Yes, Sekuru is the steward/guardian of the land you covet. Discuss your plans with him. *(Standing)* And I think now I will take something to drink from the cold room and go out and join my fellow villagers in the compound.

Pondai leaves the room to go to the cellar.

Phineas: The drive from Harare, and the jet lag from Dubai has made me drowsy. I really should go to bed now.

Pondai returns to the room.

Pondai: Did I hear you say Dubai?

Juliet: Phineas didn't tell you? We just came back from Dubai a few days ago.

Phineas: It was a little surprise trip for Juliet. She had been dying to go to Dubai.

Pondai: So how was Dubai *mukoma?*

Phineas: Expensive.

They all laugh as the ladies clear the table.

Pondai: How about Sekuru's herbal samples I sent you. Did you get a lab report on them?

Phineas: Yes let's talk about it tomorrow with him. I have not yet opened the envelope with the report but I hear it is good news.

Pondai: Ok. Let me go on to the pens to make sure Josphat closed them properly. Then I will join the community.

Pondai leaves the room.

Phineas: I am off to get some rest.

Juliet: That sounds good, but I am not tired. I will join you later. I want to go into the compound and get some fresh air and listen to the music.

Kambezo: Good night *mukoma*, get some rest.

Phineas leaves the room. Juliet and Kambezo sit in silence looking at each other.

Juliet: Now what am I going to do?

Kambezo: Meaning?

Juliet: You heard them. Phineas and his brother are opposed to our deal, so Sekuru is obviously going to oppose it too.

Kambezo: After what they have said about the road, I would not even bother bringing it up. It would be a waste of time and most probably bring us scorn from the old man.

Juliet: Yes, just what I need. A daughter-in-law who only came to "desecrate" whatever. This is ridiculous.

Kambezo: You think you got it bad, how about me the prodigal son?

Juliet puts her head in her hands as if crying.

Juliet: What is this curse that follows me? First my father dies leaving my mother, my brother and I with nothing to live on. Growing up as a child everyone said I was pretty so I thought if I showed my face to the world in beauty contests and win, some rich man would come into my life and take care of me, my mother and my brother. No, they just looked and groped and left me alone like I was a plaything. I thought I wised up and tried a different route to find some comfort in this life. It seems all my life when it seems like it's right there, it is, but it's never there. Law school was there but I dropped out because I wanted guaranteed comfort by getting married to a doctor. I did, but it is not there, it's just a fancy title of doctor's wife with just enough money to look decent. We hardly ever have any spare money. My law school classmates graduated and now they have everything I ever wanted, and I have to wait to get crumbs from their contracts when they need an errand done.

Kambezo: I am a rolling stone *mai guru*. I have gathered no moss. I have two children from two different mothers and not enough money to send any of my children to a decent school. I get tenders but I have no money to fund them, so I am just a front man. I get peanuts from the contractors. Do you know what it's like *mai guru* to go to sleep every night with your stomach empty? To wake up knowing you're just a pawn in someone else's game? To watch others, rise while you are bound to staying in the shadows? As a child, this village and *Sango reRimuka* gave me shelter and fed me when I was nothing. And now, look at me, I am back – just a man chasing scraps. I needed this deal.

Juliet sobs softly.

Juliet: There goes my office in Harare. No office, no respect, no quality paying clients.

Kambezo: *Mai guru*, you are making me feel really bad for you and of course for me. You must really want this office.

Juliet: No. It is not just an office. I want to stand on my own two feet. I do not want to wait for my ex-law school classmates to throw me a job here and there. With my own office, I can attract my own clients and charge real money for my work.

Kambezo: Maybe we can still come out of this with something.

Juliet: How? The dream is over.

Kambezo: Maybe not. I grew up with Tichaona playing in *Sango reRimuka*. We may be able to come out of this with something from there.

Juliet: Something like what?

Kambezo: I do not know, precious stones, gold nuggets, emeralds…I do not know but it's all alluvial. It's all there. The rainfall just digs up the surface and up comes all kinds of precious stones. So, if you get a small hoe or even a pointed stick, you hardly have to scratch the surface to get them.

As children Tichaona and I used to pick them and throw them at each other playing. I didn't know what it was then but now I know, I deal in gold and emeralds too, I get them from *makorokoza* and sell them saying they came from my own mine.

Juliet perks up.

Juliet: You are serious?

Kambezo: Yes. I am very serious. It's all there.

Juliet hesitates.

Juliet (*pauses, unsure*): What if they find out? What if we get caught? What will Phineas think of me? I...I wanted so much to show him that I would be more than just his wife, more than just someone with dreams that never come true.

Kambezo (*nervously*): *Mai guru* let me be honest with you. If we get caught, it won't just be Phineas we have to worry about. It won't be just Sekuru we will answer to. These villagers, they will see it as betrayal. They will never forgive us. Are you ready for that?

Juliet: I do not know but I know I need this money. I have needed it forever. As I sit here now, I see that, that forever is here and now. Can you take me there?

Kambezo: Where?

Juliet: Where the precious stones are. I want to leave this place with something. You are in the business you know where to sell them. Let us go and dig up some. The moon is shining bright in the sky we can see, can't we?

Kambezo who has been studying Juliet's face, gets up and says:

Kambezo: Yes, we can see with this moonlight alright, but *Sango reRimuka* will certainly see us too. That forest is alive, *Mai guru.* It hums when the wind passes through. It cradled me, protected me, and now, now that I have failed to make it out there in the big city, I have come back to help dig it up for its precious stones for a road to nowhere. Sometimes I wonder if it would not better if it just swallowed me whole and be done with it.

Juliet (*resolutely*): Are you changing your mind?

Kambezo: No

Juliet stands up and speaks quietly as if to herself.

Juliet: Maybe there's still a chance…(*her voice gains strength*) Maybe we can find something valuable, something that'll change everything. If *Sango reRimuka* won't give us its roads, maybe it'll give us its treasures. Kambezo, show me where the stones are. Are sure you still know your way around?

Kambezo: Certainly, *Mai guru*. I still know my way around here. No one will see us. We will get them and store them in my car.

Juliet: Ok then let me see if my husband is asleep.

Juliet leaves the room to go to the bedrooms and comes back.

Just then the people in the compound start singing loudly to the beat of thundering drums, sing:

"Mbuya Nehanda kufa vachitaura"!

Kambezo and Juliet leave the room.

CURTAIN
INTERMISSION

SANGO reRIMUKA
Does Not Eat Its Own Children

ACT Two

Scene 1

Interior. Next Day. Morning around 11 am. Sekuru Chigare Mugoti House.
When the curtain opens Zvanyadza is busy preparing food in the kitchen. She is also setting up the table in the dining room, so she is walking back and forth.
The drumming and mbira from the compound are particularly louder today because it is the day of the bira.

Juliet comes into the dining room from the bedrooms wing of the house where she had slept.

> Juliet: *Amai nini* Zvanyadza, it is practically noon time. I hope Sekuru is not up yet. It will not look good for me as his oldest *muroora* (*daughter-in-law*) to wake up so late in the day when he has been up already. I was so tired.

Zvanyadza laughs at her sister-in-law.

> Zvanyadza: Amai guru today is such a big day. Sekuru is not thinking about us, his daughters-in-law. At the moment he is meeting with the headmen and the elders of the district. I think the meeting should be ending now. *Baba mukuru* Phineas went out there to greet the elders.
> Juliet: Uhm good Sekuru won't know I just got up. (*She chuckles*) But I was so tired.

68

Juliet goes to stand by the window listening to the steady beat of the drum.

Juliet: The drum this morning is different from yesterday. It is a controlled repetitious beat. Is there a reason for that?

Zvanyadza: Yes. Today is the night of the *bira*. The drum is a reminder of the occasion. Yesterday it was just fun but today the drumming is a message.

Juliet: Oh, very interesting.

Pondai and Rudo enter the room with two baskets filled with eggs.

Pondai: Good morning *mai guru*. How are feeling this morning?

Rudo: Good morning aunty.

Juliet: Good morning to you two. I just need some tea or coffee so I can wake up. *(She exclaims)* Oh my! Look at all those eggs. Where did you get them from? Sekuru's patients? *(She laughs).*

Rudo: You could say that, but we collect them from our chickens. We have many, many chickens in the henhouse.

Juliet: Henhouse? Where is that?

Pondai: You must see it, but today there is too much going on out there. Remind me to give you a tour before you go back to Harare.

Pondai turns to Rudo.

Pondai: Rudo go and get us empty cartoons for our eggs so we can pack them and put them away.

Rudo leaves the room to get the egg cartons.

Juliet: This is serious business. What do you do with all these eggs?

Pondai: We pack them in egg cartons for sale and distribution through the shops at Sadza township.

Juliet: About how many dozens of eggs do you take to the township when you go?

Pondai: It depends on the hens but on average we take about 30 cartoons. Each carton carries a dozen eggs.

Juliet: Really? That's a lot of eggs. I am impressed by the way you do things in this village.

Rudo returns with an armful of empty egg cartoons.

Juliet: So Rudo, what about Elton and Chipo? Where are they?

Rudo: I do not know. I thought they were here.

Juliet: Not in this house, there are not here. *Baba mudiki* Pondai, have you seen the children?

Pondai: I do not think I have. I last saw them yesterday when the three of them left to go pick berries in *Sango reRimuka*.

Zvanyadza: I have not seen them either, but I have not been anywhere. I am busy with preparations for the *bira*. I do not have much time.

Juliet: Did they sleep at your house?

Rudo: We ended up playing hide and seek in the forest but I ran home and hid in mum and dad's bed and fell asleep. So, I do not know. I woke up with dad to come here and do coding as we do every Monday morning.

Pondai: Yes, we do coding lessons on Mondays, but Chipo does not always come to the lessons.

Juliet: So where did they sleep? You are not worried? Where could they be?

Zvanyadza *(laughing)*: They slept somewhere, either in this house or our house. There is nothing to worry about. They are around somewhere.

Juliet: Elton should come in and wash up and change his clothes.

Pondai: They will come in at some point, here in the village children do not stay indoors. They play all day out in the yard or the forest. We let them come and go whenever.

Juliet: Uhm I do not know. Where could they be if you did not see them at your house?

Pondai: Let me ask Josphat, he tends the animals, so he is in and out of the village compound. He is everywhere where the animals may go.

Pondai goes to the open window and shouts.

Pondai: Josphat! Josphat!

Voice: Yes *baba*.

Pondai: Josphat have you seen Chipo and her cousin?

Voice: Yes sir. They are in *Sango reRimuka*. I saw them when I was coming from the river a while ago.

Pondai: Alright. Thank you.

Pondai turns to Juliet with a smile.

Pondai: You see, there is nothing to worry about.

Zvanyadza: I knew they were out there somewhere. When they are hungry, they will come in.

Phineas comes into the house holding a DHL package envelop.

Phineas: Good morning *amai va* Elton, you slept well?

Juliet: Yes, just a little tired.

Phineas: Coffee always pecks you up. (*To Zvanyadza*) *Amai nini* is the coffee ready. I smell the aroma.

Zvanyadza: Two coffees coming up.

Phineas takes a seat alongside Juliet and hands the DHL envelop to Pondai.

Phineas *(laughing):* When I went to the car to get the envelop, I saw Kambezo still fast asleep in his car.

Pondai: Maybe Kambezo danced so much in the compound late last night after we left. If it had been me, I would not wake up until next week.

Phineas: You would be surprised as a musician working in night clubs, he is used to late nights.

Pondai leaves the egg packaging to Rudo and rips open the DHL package and starts reading the documents in the envelop.

As Zvanyadza comes back from the kitchen with the coffee for Phineas and Juliet, Pondai continues to read the documents.

Pondai puts the documents down and looks up at his brother and asks.

Pondai: *Mukoma* I see the return address is from New York in America.

Phineas: Yes, I sent the sample herb plants to my friend in New York.

Pondai: *Mukoma* do you know what's in these documents?

Phineas: I am not sure. I did not open it. It arrived at the house day before yesterday and I thought that since this is your project, I would just bring the envelop here and let you deal with whatever is in it. What are they saying?

Pondai: Did you receive a US$50,000 wire transfer to your bank account?

Phineas: Right now, I do not know, but I was told there is a consulting fee that my friend Mukiwa, the VP pharmacologist in New York is organizing for me.

Juliet: Honey, have you checked your account, there may be the $50,000 in it?

Phineas: No, I haven't. I did not know that he had sent me any money. All I know is he sent me the tickets to Dubai.

Juliet: The tickets to Dubai were from someone else? I thought you bought them for us.

Phineas: Ah *Amai va* Elton be serious, do you know how much those first-class airline tickets and the five star hotel accommodations cost?

Pondai: *Mukoma* the $50,000 and the tickets to Dubai were for you to do what?

Phineas: To be a consultant on projects that he is putting together.

Pondai: You got paid to work on *Sango reRimuka.*

Phineas: To work on *Sango reRimuka* doing what? What happened is that instead of sending Sekuru's herbal samples you gave me to a local lab in Harare, I decided to send them to Mukiwa because they have bigger and better facilities in New York than here. He was just supposed to provide an analysis for the labelling and to give me a quotation of the costs.

Pondai: *Mukoma*, Mukiwa has hired you to work as a consultant for his pharmaceutical company to assist in the acquisition of *Sango reRimuka*, the land where these herbal samples came from.

Phineas: What?

Pondai: Here it is in black and white, right here. The full document says that they estimate the purchase price for the forest as 10 million US dollars to be paid once x number of samples have been received. Full title of the forest will mean that it will be fenced off for security reasons, but locals will be allowed in on a restricted basis and they will get all the jobs.

Furthermore, you will be paid $2 million dollars as an agent of the company if you peg a mining claim in the forest which their mining subsidiary company will develop.

Juliet jumps from her chair shouting.

Juliet: We are rich! Rich! Rich! Rich! 10 million dollars! 2 million dollars! Doctor Phineas Mugoti, you are a very, very rich man.

Juliet is besides herself with excitement.

Phineas: Juliet! Please sit down! No one is rich here!

Juliet: What do you mean no one is rich? These documents are talking about 10 million US dollars. 2 million US dollars from America. And right now, there is probably $50,000 in your bank account right now just sitting there! What do you mean, no one is rich?

Phineas: Get this through your head. I do not know what got into Mukiwa. What he is saying is rubbish. No one is selling *Sango reRimuka*.

Juliet: Why not? The price is good and very high. You want a higher price?

Phineas: Juliet please be quiet. Obviously, you have no clue about what's going on here.

Juliet: Yes, I will admit, it seems I have no clue on what's going on; but I can assure you that even little Rudo here understands that you are being offered 12 million U S dollars to help ourselves have a better life. My friend Melania changes cars every two years. She takes trips to London, Dubai and everywhere. For me, for us, I have just found out that we could not even afford the trip to Dubai I was bragging about. Life is about money. It is about the-haves and the-have-not. I am tired of being the have-not. You are being offered 12 million dollars right here, right now. I have a clue about that.

Phineas: I keep telling you Juliet, not everything is about money.

Juliet: If it is not about money, then what is it about?

Phineas: In this case it is about independence and the common good. If we agree to this ridiculous offer, it means the people of the 20 villages will no longer enjoy the life they have. They will now have to depend on some big foreign company for jobs.

Juliet: But they will have jobs.

Phineas: Jobs being paid chicken feed. And what happens after they have extracted what they want from the land? The jobs will disappear. Or better yet, can your child inherit your job when you die? Juliet it is obvious to me you have no idea of the consequences of what this proposal means to the people who live here.

Phineas is trying to control his anger. He speaks through his clenched teeth.

Phineas: Rudo, go into that bedroom and get my phone. I am going to straighten this nonsense right now. Hurry up.

Pondai: As I am reading this, I realize that these people do not know who we are.

Phineas: Just wait.

Juliet is quiet, crest fallen.
Rudo gives Phineas the phone.
Phineas calls Mukiwa in New York. He puts the phone on speaker
so everyone in the room can hear the conversation.

Voice: Hello Phineas. Mukiwa here. Did you finally open the DHL package? Yesterday when we talked, you said you had not yet read the proposals we sent you. We are anxious to get the ball rolling.

Phineas: I have not read any of it but my younger brother Pondai the one who gave me the samples I sent you has read it. Pondai is studying bioengineering.

Voice: I remember Pondai, even as a young boy when we were at university, he used to send you his school report cards - all A's, always. Anyway, how is he? And how are the preparations for the *bira* going?

Phineas: All was well until just now when I was told what you are proposing. Are you mad? Have you gone crazy?

Voice: What? What's wrong?

Phineas: Everything is wrong, that's what. We have been friends since before I got married. You know my family history, what would make you think that I would participate in any of this? Sell

Sango reRimuka. Peg mining claims in the sacred forest. What has got into you?

Voice: Slow down. Slow down Phineas. We are friends and have always been. I am in a big, big world and things have changed. So, I thought you and your family may have changed too?

Phineas: I have no idea about the 50,000 you said you wired to my account, and it cannot have anything to do with *Sango reRimuka.* I will send it back.

Juliet: What? Send it back? Why?

Phineas: Hushhhh.

Voice: Slow down Phineas, you are my friend. I would not ask you to do anything that is against your ethics and morals for 50,000 dollars. MCK Pharma is a multibillion-dollar corporation. 50,000 dollars is like 50 dollars to you. No one is going to miss that. It came from my petty cash box.

Phineas: I do not want it if it compromises my family.

Voice: No one is compromising your family. Let me explain.

Phineas: Go ahead.

Voice: I oversee worldwide procurement of raw materials for my company. Climate change has upended our locations throughout the world where we were growing our own trees and plants from which we extract the active ingredient in our pain pills especially for headaches and migraines. The sample you sent me was the purest form for the active ingredient we need for our most popular and most profitable brand. I did not tell the lab techs where the sample was from, even though we did not sign a non-disclosure form. I knew that identifying where I got the sample from would bring you untold and unwanted attention until you and I had a deal. So, no harm has been done. I was just looking for a source for our raw materials. The proposal I sent you is a standard agreement we use in Laos, Brazil everywhere in the world. Of course, we tweak it but its standard.

Phineas: And the gold claim stuff?

Voice: It so happens that through experience we have found that whenever certain vegetation is located there is usually some precious minerals there especially gold. So again, it was nothing personal. It was just a business proposition.

Phineas: Now about the 50,000 dollars. I signed that electronic document before you sent me the tickets to Dubai. I do not have a copy of the electronic document here, where can I get a copy? What did I sign?

Voice: You signed on to help us as a consultant in South Central Africa to identify opportunities to source raw materials. *Sango reRimuka* does not have to be a part of it.

Phineas: Ok.

Voice: If I can speak to your younger brother Pondai in the future I can be a consultant to him as he tries to move Sekuru's migraine headache herbal supplement. I may live in New York, but I am a Zimbabwean at heart and proud of it. I want to help grow the industry if I can.

Phineas: Pondai happens to be here. You want to speak to him?

Voice: Yes please.

Pondai: Hello Dr Kwezi.

Voice: I am your brother's best friend. Call me *mukoma*. I like what you are trying to do.

Pondai: Thank you *mukoma*.

Voice: I know the local specifications needed to get Sekuru's product in the pharmacies as a complementary medicine.

Pondai: Yes, I have done the research, herbal supplements can be sold in pharmacies here as long as you can provide the specifics of what the active ingredients are, colorations and type of capsule packaging. That is what I was hoping *mukoma* Phineas could get for me.

Voice: Consider it done. There is a local lab there in Harare that I trust. I will put you together with them.

Pondai: Thank you, *mukoma*.

Voice: Ok Phineas my friend, enjoy the *bira* and regards to Sekuru. He is no charlatan. I am so proud of him.

Phineas. Bye we will talk later.

Phineas and Pondai high five each other.

Phineas: I would never betray my family legacy and trust for $50,000 or any kind of money. That $50,000 will go into setting up the business to package Sekuru's herbal supplements for migraine headaches! Yippy! This Heroes holiday weekend is turning out to be something special! *(He turns to Zvanyadza) Mai nini* what are we feasting on today to celebrate comrade Tichaona our hero? A double celebration!

Zvanyadza (*ululates while Pondai claps his hands*): Mupawose! *Gamba!* Comrade Tichaona bringer of good luck! We have prepared beef, goat meat, chicken, peanut butter veggies, peanut butter rice whatever you want we have it!

Rudo: How about a cake?

Zvanyadza: Uhm yes of course, what kind of a celebration of our comrade Tichaona would it be without cake?

Rudo: Yes, yes, yes mummy!

Juliet has lost all the joy and excitement that had come with the million-dollar proposal. She stands up and says:

Juliet: I am going to go look for Elton. Rudo come and show me where Elton and Chipo are.

Rudo: Yes aunty.

Juliet: Get a bag from the kitchen. I want to collect *matowhe.*

Phineas: Bring *mazhanje* too (*chuckling*).

Juliet is down cast. She has something on her mind.

As Juliet and Rudo exit into the compound, the sounds of the drumming and the people enjoying themselves come into the house through the open door.

Sekuru Mugoti enters the room. He is a tall regal figure. He wears an all-black outfit. He wears bangles on both his arms and holds a walking stick that marks his authority. He is beaming with a smile as he takes his seat at the head of the table.

They all stand when he enters the room and clap their hands as they greet him. They sit down after he sits.

Pondai: Good morning Mupawose

Sekuru: Good morning Mupawose. I am glad to see you are all up.

Phineas: Heroes Day is not the time to sleep *baba*.

Sekuru: That's right Mupawose.

Pondai continues to pack the eggs into the cartons alone now that Rudo has gone with Juliet.

Zvanyadza appears from the kitchen with a teapot and a cup.

Zvanyadza: Sekuru I do not know, the tea may not be as hot anymore.

Sekuru: Do not worry about that *mai* Chipo. It is my fault. I am an old man. I talk too much when my fellow old men come here. I should have come back in the house sooner, but we had not seen each other in a while.

Zvanyadza: It is not a problem Sekuru just let me know. I am preparing your favourite dish of veggies and peanut butter brown rice.

Sekuru: What would we do without you *muroora?*

They all laugh as Sekuru pours himself a cup of tea.

Kambezo, who is not as care free and as bubbly as he was yesterday, walks in.

Kambezo: Knock, knock. May we came in?

Phineas: Come in, come in, Kambezo.

When Kambezo sees Sekuru sitting at the table he squats and claps his hands, respectfully.

Kambezo: Mupawose, *mhuka huru. Makadiyiko (how are you, Your Highness)?*

Sekuru puts his cup down and smiles looking at Kambezo:

Sekuru: Kambezo my son, you have come to celebrate your friend and brother Tichaona our fallen comrade?

Kambezo: *Hongu* (yes) Sekuru.

Sekuru: Get up and come and sit here at the table. *Mai* Chipo will give you a cup so we can share this tea.

Kambezo: Thank you Sekuru, let me sit over here on the sofa.

Zvanyadza brings Kambezo a cup.

Zvanyadza: Good afternoon *baba mukuru.*

Kambezo: *Mai nini* thank you.

Kambezo is clearly uncomfortable. He sits on a sofa away from the table. His demeanour sombre, unlike the funny guy from the previous day.

Phineas: I saw you sound asleep in your car.

Kambezo: I was not asleep *mukoma.* I just did not know how I would be able to come back into this house after what I did last night.

Phineas: You did not do anything outrageous. You were just funny as usual.

Pondai: *Mukoma* you did not do anything.

85

Kambezo: Yes, I did. I did something that is shameful and disrespectful to this village that I grew up in.

Sekuru: Whatever it is, the fact that you are talking about it is a sign of innocence and maturity. What is it my son? You will be forgiven.

Kambezo: I hope so Sekuru. I thought *vadzimu* had given me a chance to do big business. I came here on a mission to ask you to change your mind about the road through *Sango reRimuka*.

Sekuru: Ok go on.

Kambezo: I arrived yesterday full of dreams of the riches that we were going to get when we convince you to allow the road through *Sango reRimuka* to be built. I am part of the company that wants to build these roads in Sadza District.

Sekuru: There is nothing wrong with being in a company. That is how you hunt these days, a company is your spear to chase after the big animals in business.

Kambezo: Sekuru *amai guru* Juliet and I are working on it together.

Sekuru: Ok go on.

Kambezo: Yesterday we spent the whole afternoon in this room talking with Pondai and *mukoma* Phineas trying to persuade them to see the benefit of the road. They stood firm and told us that a road through *Sango reRimuka* would be disastrous for the villages and that you, as the steward/guardian of the *Sango reRimuka*, would never allow it.

Sekuru: That is true.

Kambezo: Sekuru I must say, I must not have been myself, I was not thinking straight. Later on, in the night after you had gone to bed *mukoma* Phineas, and Pondai and his wife had also gone to their house, something must have got into my spirit to do the unthinkable. Maybe it is just greed. Wanting money. I do not know. It was just me and *Mai guru* Juliet trying to think of what to do with our business, but we saw no way forward. Anyway, *Mai guru* Juliet was sad and crying, mourning the fact that the deal was not going to happen because if your two sons would not even consider the idea then there was no chance that you, yourself, Sekuru would want to even talk about it. She was quite upset. So, I told her that Tichaona and I know *Sango reRimuka* inside out and I could show her where gold nuggets, emeralds and other precious stones wash up on the surface of the soil. I told her I knew where we could dig them up from the topsoil. I told her it was easy. Well, that quietened her down. With all that singing and dancing that was going on in the compound, I knew that no one would pay us any mind. It so happened that I had an empty sack in my car. We went to my car and took the sack. Since I know where you keep the tools, I found a hoe there and took it. Then we disappeared from the compound and went into *Sango reRimuka*. We collected and dug up quite a number of different precious stones. The moon was bright but not bright enough for me to distinguish one precious stone from another, but I knew they were all worth a lot of money. After that we came back with our precious stones. I kept the sack and took it to my car, and she came back into the house to sleep.

Pondai: Uhm so you have them in your car?

Kambezo: No. Sometime early this morning I am not sure whether I was dreaming or just my spirit being restless. I saw Tichaona in a dream. I am not sure, but I think he asked me how I was. I think I said I was well. Then he asked me why I was doing what I had done. Why did I want to bring destruction to *Sango reRimuka* because I would have to explain where I got all those precious stones to sell them. Then I think I woke up. I sat up and knew that I had to return everything. I could not keep anything not even one stone.

Phineas: Uhm quite a story.

Kambezo: I just took the sack full of the precious stones back and emptied it there where I had found them, spreading them all over. Sekuru please forgive me. I do not know what had got into me. I am not a thief.

Sekuru: There is nothing wrong. All is well. You returned what belonged to *Sango reRimuka* to *Sango reRimuka*. You have not betrayed the secrets of *Sango reRimuka*. All is well.

Kambezo: I am ashamed because after all these years, I came back and did what I did. You took me as your own and raised me with Tichaona as your own son. (*He starts crying.*) I cannot repay you like this.

Sekuru: No harm was done. Have some tea or something to calm you down. We are grateful you are a son of this village. Good things are coming into your life. Keep working and trying, that is all one can do.

Pondai stands up to break the tension in the room and announces.

Pondai: All the eggs are packed now let me see if I can carry them to the storeroom without dropping one.

Kambezo: Let me help you with that.

As Pondai stands, the door opens. In rushes Elton and Chipo shouting. Pondai and Kambezo exit the room with the egg cartons and return.

Elton & Chipo: Sekuru! Sekuru! Sekuru!

They rush to Sekuru and they both hug him. Sekuru embraces them.

Elton & Chipo (*talking together*): Sekuru, sekuru wait till we tell what we did!

Sekuru: Ok one at a time. Sit down…

Zvanyadza looks at them and sees they have mud on their clothes and faces.

Zvanyadza: Sekuru let them tell their story quickly standing up, they will soil the chairs. They need to wash up before Aunty Juliet sees Elton looking like he has been rolling in the mud like a pig.

Everyone laughs.

Sekuru: So, tell me what happened?

Everyone is smiling staring at the Elton and Chipo as they began to tell their story.

Elton: Me first. Sekuru yesterday we were playing in the forest. Rudo was there too. We were playing *chiwande wande* (hide and seek).

Chipo: But we could not find Rudo.

Elton: I think she went home.

Sekuru: One at a time. Tell me the story.

Eton: When we could not find Rudo, we were just playing around when Chipo and I noticed a bird nest that had fallen from a tree.

Chipo: And Sekuru, the tiny, tiny little birds were just lying there with their mouths open.

Elton: It was so sad. Sekuru, you taught us that no one is allowed to hunt birds in *Sango reRimuka*...

Chipo: Because they are so small there is no meat on them it's just a waste of life to kill birds.

Elton: And they help the forest like bees do.

Sekuru: That is correct.

Elton: It was getting dark, and the little things were crying for their mother. So Chipo said let's rebuild their nest and put them back in it.

Chipo: But it was getting dark, and we could not see.

Elton: So, we decided to take them with us so the other animals would not eat them.

Chipo: We slept with them in our room, but we built a home for them with cardboard which I found where *baba* keeps his tools.

Elton: We did not want them to make any noise, so we fed them.

Chipo: I went in the kitchen and found some grains and some water, and we fed them.

Elton: So early, early this morning before anyone was awake, we brought them back *to Sango reRimuka*, to the tree and rebuilt their nest.

Chipo: And I climbed up the tree and put the nest where it had fallen from.

Sekuru: How did you know it was the right tree and the right sport.

Chipo: There were bird feathers and straw in the tree branch that we could see even standing on the ground.

Elton: Then we saw my mother and Rudo come to the forest but we did not want them to come where we were sitting. We did not want anyone to come to the tree because it would scare aware the mother bird.

Sekuru: Then what happened?

Elton: You know how you always say if you are quiet in *Sango reRimuka* and wish something good to happen, it will happen?

Sekuru: Yes.

Chipo: So, Elton and I sat quietly under the tree thinking and wishing hard for the mother bird to come back to her children.

Sekuru: And? Did she come?

Elton & Chipo (*clapping their hands*); Yes, she came! She came!   It worked! Sekuru, it worked! We wished hard and it worked! The little birds and their mother are happy again!

Sekuru, Phineas, Pondai, Kambezo, Zvanyadza all clap their hands saying:

Sekuru: Very good. I am proud of you.

Zvanyadza: Now run along and wash up and change into clean clothes before Aunty Juliet comes back and finds you looking like this!

Elton: Do not worry, she did not see us, but we saw her, and we ran away back to the house before she could find us.

Zvanyadza: Alright now run along and do as I told you.

Elton: Yes, yes we are going.

Kambezo stands up from the sofa and says:

Kambezo: I too must go and clean up. I have a change of clothes in the car.

Pondai: You know *mukoma* Kambezo, we have an indoor bathroom in here. Last night you kept going outside, I did not say anything because you wanted to go to your car to get your water but there is a bathroom in here.

Kambezo laughs.

Kambezo: Thank you. But I will use the outhouse, there is a bucket to get water from the well, so I will be ok. And please allow me to add something

93

about last night. None of what happened was *Mai guru* Juliet's fault. She did not ask me to do anything. I am the one who had the idea. She just followed me.

Sekuru: All is well my son. Be at peace. Today we celebrate your friend and brother Comrade Tichaona our own national liberation hero. That is all that is important.

Kambezo: Yes sir! Thank you Sekuru. I thank you all.

Kambezo exits the room,

Sekuru: Oh my, so much going here. I am glad Kambezo returned those things back to their owners out there. But my grandchildren make me proud. They will take care of our future. I am so happy about their little story..

Before Sekuru could finish what he is saying, his words are drowned by a high pitched shrill sound coming from the sky. The sound of a horde of crow birds shrieking in the air rises eerily above the din of the drums. The shriek of the crows grows louder and louder but the sound of the steady beat of the drum does not change. The shriek of the crows reaches a crescendo as Juliet bursts through the door back into the house with Rudo behind her. In her hand is the hat that she had Elton wear yesterday when he and the twins went to play in Sango reRimuka. She is hysterical. She is crying and screaming with her body shaking all over. People from the compound have followed her, they look into the house through the open windows shouting; "What is it? What is it? What is she running from?"

Juliet *(hysterical):* Phineas! Phineas our child is in grave danger! Elton may be dead as we speak! Look here is his hat!

Pondai *(getting up from the chair):* What are you talking about?

Juliet: The children may be dead in the forest as we speak! Oh my God! My son is dead!

Juliet is screaming and for a moment everyone is stunned. They cannot make sense of what she is saying. Phineas gets up from his chair puts his arms around her.

Phineas: Please tell us what is happening to you.

Juliet: It's not what's happening to me that you should be worried about. It is the children! They cannot possibly survive those lions and tigers in *Sango reRimuka* where they went.

Pondai: Lions and tigers?

Juliet: Yes, lions, tigers, hyenas, jackals! Anything with teeth that eats people is out there. I saw them! How could my son have survived that? Here is his hat! Elton is dead! *(She shouts.)* Phineas! *(Turning to Pondai)* Pondai, please, please go with your brother and take some men with you and go see about the children. I just know it. My son is

95

dead. I lost three children in miscarriages and now this! To lose Elton to wild animals like that!

Sekuru clears his throat to get everyone's attention.

Sekuru: Pondai go the window and tell people to go back to what they we are doing. Tell them I said everything is in order.

Pondai goes to the window and shouts.

Pondai: Play the drums and celebrate! Sekuru said the ancestors have spoken. All is in order.

Phineas: The children are safe. But you better tell Sekuru what happed.

Juliet: No, I want you Phineas and some men to go get what is left of my son.

Pondai: *Mai guru,* Sekuru is the steward and guardian of *Sango reRimuka,* no man goes in there armed unless Sekuru says so. Slow down and tell him so he can do as you ask.

Juliet: You all think I am crazy? I know what I saw and Rudo and I are lucky we were not eaten.

Sekuru, Phineas, Pondai, Zvanyadza and Rudo exchange quizzical looks. No one can understand why Juliet is in the state she is in because they all know that Elton and Chipo are safe in the house washing themselves off.

Juliet finally sits down in a chair next to her husband still crying.

Sekuru *(ignoring Juliet's crying):* Welcome *muroora*. It has been a long time since you visited us.

Juliet is unsure of herself. She tries to speak through muffled crying but breaks down.

Sekuru: Do not cry *muroora*, *Amai va* Elton. There is only peace here. Today we are here to celebrate your brother-in-law Tichaona. What could the matter be?

Juliet: My son Sekuru. My son is in grave danger. He may be dead.

Sekuru: Think about it. If Elton was in grave danger, would his father and uncle Pondai be just sitting there? Would I be sitting here talking to you?

Juliet: But he may be dead. No one can survive all those wild animals.

Sekuru: What wild animals?

Juliet: In *Sango reRimuka*, they wanted to eat us.

Sekuru: *Amai va* Elton, *muroora*, *Sango reRimuka* does not eat its own children.

Juliet: There are there. Lions, hyenas, tigers, and I do not know what else is out there. Rudo and I barely escaped with our lives.

Sekuru: I just told you. *Sango reRimuka* does not eat its own children. Rudo was with you?

Juliet: Yes

Sekuru turns to Rudo who is sitting with her mother wide-eyed trying to comprehend what is happening with Aunty Juliet.

Sekuru: Rudo, *muzukuru (grandchild)*.

Rudo: Yes Sekuru?

Sekuru: Rudo, did you go with *amai guru* to *Sango reRimuka*?

Rudo: Yes

Sekuru: What happened?

Rudo: Nothing. I saw Elton and Chipo sitting on the grass under a tree. I was about to run to them when *mai guru* started screaming and grabbed my hand and said run. So, I just ran behind her.

Sekuru: Did you see anything there that you do not see every day when you go to play and pick berries in *Sango reRimuka*.

Rudo: No.

Juliet: But we saw lions and tigers.

Rudo: Maybe but I did not see them because I was looking at Elton and Chipo.

Sekuru: Oh, very well.

Sekuru turns back to Juliet who is quietly sobbing.

Sekuru: As I told you. *Sango reRimuka* does not eat its own children. Why do you want to harm the forest? What has it done to you?

The question throws Juliet off her self-pity.

Juliet: Excuse me Sekuru I did not hear you.

Sekuru: I asked you. Why do you want to harm the forest?

Juliet: I do not want to harm anyone.

Sekuru: Why is *Sango reRimuka* defending itself against you?

Juliet: Defend itself against me? I have not done anything to it.

Sekuru: You last came here five years ago when you came to bury Phineas' mother, your mother-in-law. You have not been here since. Phineas and Elton come home all the time and nothing has ever happened to Elton.

Juliet: I am afraid of spiders and insects and wild animals that's why I do not come with them.

Sekuru: I want you to know that no matter what and or how you came, we are happy to see you *Amai va* Elton, you are precious to us, you are part of our family, this is your home too. But why did you come to visit us this time? Is it the *bira?*

Juliet stops crying abruptly. She is clearly uncomfortable. She stammers in her speech.

Juliet: I just decided to come. It's Heroes Holiday weekend, I did not want to be alone at the house in Harare.

Sekuru: Is that all?

Juliet: Yes.

Sekuru: *Amai va* Elton if you love your child as you say you do, you better tell me everything. Why is *Sango reRimuka* defending itself against you. It sent all those powerful animals to keep you out.

Juliet: But my son...

Sekuru: There are three people living today who will meet no harm in *Sango reRimuka* no matter what. Those three people are myself because I am the first-born son of my father. Phineas your husband, because he is my first-born son. And Elton because he is the first-born son of his father, Phineas. Each first born of our family, Mugoti Family, in each generation becomes the steward and guardian of *Sango reRimuka*. That is why each one of us is called *Gamba* reRimuka. If I or my son or grandson Elton were to harbour any harmful thoughts about *Sango reRimuka* we would not die in there, we would just get lost and not come out until we repent, and rituals have been done to cleanse us. *Sango reRimuka* would never let any harm come to Elton. He is safe right here in the house.

Silence.

Sekuru: So, you see, Elton is not dead as you say. The tears you are crying, you should be crying for yourself because you cannot win the war you want to bring against *Sango reRimuka*.

Juliet starts crying again and speaks through her tears.

Juliet: I have not done anything to harm *Sango reRimuka*. I just want my son back.

Sekuru: Your son is not there. He is not dead. But I ask you again, besides the *bira* or anything else, why did you come with Phineas and Elton to visit us after all this time?

Juliet goes into a deep sorrowful bout of sobbing uncontrollably.

Sekuru: What is it? You cannot win. The forces against you are mightier than you can imagine. It is all our ancestors' spirits who live in that *Sango reRimuka* that you are trying to tangle with.

Juliet finally simmers down and starts talking hesitantly.

Juliet: Sekuru, *baba*, I had no idea. I just wanted to have my own business representing businesses and organizations that want to do projects. If I had known I would be sacrificing my son, my only Elton, I would have never agreed to it.

Sekuru: What business is that?

Juliet: I have a business in public relations. I get small projects to help organizations and businesses. But with this one I was going to make enough money to have my own offices and staff.

Sekuru: What did you do that has brought on all the ancestors to fight you.

Juliet: Some people from the Sadza District Council and some investors and a mining company representative came to see me in Harare in secret. They decided to use a road construction company to enter Sadza District but with the intention of coming to *Sango reRimuka*. We met at a lawyer's office, the lawyer who hired me on behalf of the investors. There was a man I had never met, who comes from this village, his name is Kambezo. He grew up here. He came with the road construction company. We agreed to come to see you this hero's weekend to convince you to let the road construction company build a road in *Sango reRimuka*.

Sekuru: Uhmm did they pay you?

Juliet: We signed some papers; I came out here to see for myself and work out the plan. I was paid an engagement fee. I will get paid more at our next meeting.

Sekuru: Did your husband know about this?

Juliet. No.

Sekuru: *Muroora,* do you know who you have joined up with?

Juliet: Yes, no. I am not sure.

Sekuru: You have entered a world, a dangerous place, my daughter. There will be repercussions because these people will not go away and now, they have you.

Juliet starts crying again.

> Juliet: Punish me, not my son. I do not care about the business. I want my son back in my arms. I do not care what happens to me. My son is innocent.
> Sekuru: Nothing will happen to your son. Nothing happened to your son.
> Juliet: I saw what I saw, I am not mad.
> Sekuru: No one is questioning what you saw but Elton is innocent, he has no ill will towards *Sango reRimuka*. Elton and Chipo are here with us. No harm came to him and no harm will come to him. I do not know about you.
>
> *(Sekuru pauses with his eyes set on Juliet.)*
>
> Kambezo is a son of this village. He confessed and told us how he took you to *Sango reRimuka* to dig up precious stones last night. He told us everything, he confessed, and returned the stones, and he is forgiven. But you? What are you hiding?

Juliet continues crying.

> Juliet: I am so ashamed. I made a bad situation worse. This afternoon *Baba va* Elton had an opportunity to make money with his friend in America by selling *Sango reRimuka*. When he refused the offer of the millions of dollars that he was being offered, I got angry. I could not help it. I decided to go back to *Sango reRimuka* to dig up

more gold nuggets and everything I could find to add to what we had collected last night with Kambezo. I took Rudo with me, I was going to let her play with Elton and Chipo while I did what I wanted to do. I did not want to pick any *matowhe* or *mazhanje*. I just wanted precious stones. But when we got to the edge of the *Sango reRimuka* that is when the animals started coming at me to eat me.

Juliet is now sobbing loudly.

Juliet: *Baba va* Elton, Phineas, my husband please forgive me. I do not know what got into me. You know how much I love our son.

Phineas stands up and stands behind Juliet with his hands on her shoulders consoling her.

Phineas: I know that, but you must have an honest conversation with Sekuru. May be he can advise us how to navigate your way out of whatever is driving you.

Juliet: Sekuru I know it was the love of money but honestly, I do not really care about the money, about going to Dubai or buying new cars every two years. I do not care about all that. I do not want the riches of *Sango reRimuka*, I just want my son back.

Sekuru: You have not accepted what we keep telling you that your son is safe and is here in the house only because you are lost in the grip of your own guilt.

Zvanyadza stands up also and comes to console and advise Juliet.

Zvanyadza: *Amai guru* Juliet, Sekuru does not volunteer to help anyone. He only helps those who genuinely ask for help. Ask Sekuru how you can help yourself get rid of whatever guilt it is you are feeling.

Juliet: I am so ashamed. I have embarrassed my husband in front of his family. How do I ask for forgiveness? I should have left this matter about the road into *Sango reRimuka* alone yesterday especially after *Baba mudiki* Pondai explained why *Sango reRimuka* should never be touched by a bulldozer or grader. But no, I did not. I just wanted what I wanted for myself so I could brag to my ex-law school classmates who have their own practices. It was all for vanity. As I sit here I realize I do not want to go to Dubai or to fly to New York. I just want my family. I want my son in my arms. I lost three children in miscarriages. I can never have another. I want Elton back in my arms. My husband makes enough money to take care of us.

Elton and Chipo enter the room from the bedroom wing of the house where they had washed themselves and changed into clean clothes. Juliet with her head down still sobbing does not see Elton come and lift her face.

Elton: Mummy why are you crying?

Juliet is surprised to see Elton.

Juliet: Elton my son, you are alive. You are safe.

Elton: Why are you crying mummy. Is something wrong? It's Uncle Comrade Tichaona's day why are you crying? Did I do something wrong?

Juliet: No son. This is the happiest day of my life. I am crying because I am happy.

Juliet holding Elton tightly, wipes off her tears.

Juliet turns to Sekuru.

Juliet: Sekuru I am asking for your help. I want this family unity and happiness to last forever. I do not want to ever lose my son again.

Sekuru: *Muroora*, go back to *Sango reRimuka.* Your husband and son, Elton will take you there. They are the heirs of *Sango reRimuka.* Go and pick the fruits and berries of its trees, pick *matowhe* and *mazhange* and bring us some too. All will be well. Be at peace with nature. Be at peace with the land you stand on.

Elton: Yeees! I am going back to *Sango reRimuka*. Come mummy I want to show you the bird nest that Chipo and I built. Come let's go!

Phineas helps Juliet get up from the chair. Phineas, Juliet and Elton exit the room.

CURTAIN

THE END

GLOSSARY